BDSM Master/slave Contract

This book and its contents are for entertainment purposes only. This is not a legally binding contract. Warning - *Even if a Spanking and/or BDSM contract is not considered legally binding in your country/locality, attempts may be made to include parts of it in law enforcement or other legal proceedings, should their involvement ever occur for some reason. "Consent" could be a defense to assault in many places (though not necessarily effective.) A legal argument might be attempted stating that by signing the contract you are agreeing to everything in it. Also, in areas of the world where some or all BDSM activities are illegal, contracts of any sort can be used to prosecute those involved.*

This book is sold and/or distributed with the understanding that the publisher and author is not engaged in rendering legal or other professional services. This book and its subject matter is for entertainment purposes only. In this publication there may be inadvertent inaccuracies including technical inaccuracies, typographical inaccuracies and other possible inaccuracies. **The writer and publisher of this publication expressly disclaim all liability for the use or interpretation by anybody of information contained in this publication.** The author, publisher and distributors of this publication hereby disclaim any and all liability for any loss or damage caused by errors or omissions resulted from negligence, accident, or any other causes. If legal advice or other expert assistance is required, the services of a competent professional person in a consultation capacity should be sought. Products, services and websites' content vary with time. Please verify any published information.

ISBN-13: 978-1482552676
ISBN-10: 1482552671

Erotic BDSM Books - Your Erotic BDSM Book Publisher
EroticBDSMbooks.com

Other BDSM Books by Phil G. Include:

**Mistress/slave BDSM Contract*
**The Absolutely Essential Book of BDSM and S&M Rules*
**Things To Do During 3 Hours of Sex; A Step-by-step Guide*
**Playtime At The Dom Den; A Step-by-step Guide*
**The Absolutely Essential Guide to Great BDSM and S&M Sex*
**The Absolutely Essential Dominant/submissive Playtime Experience*
**The Absolutely Essential BDSM Sexual Experience*
**The Ultimate Collection of S&M and BDSM Rules For Female Submissives and Slaves*
**Master and submissive or slave BDSM Contract*
**The Funniest BDSM Personal Ads*
**Have Awesome BDSM Sex*
**Spanking Dictionary*
**Spanking Contract*
**BDSM Rules*
**Bed Arrest, the Punishment for BDSM Enthusiasts*

Table of Contents

Introduction

Please read the contract carefully as in many cases the default language of the contract is set up to not allow certain specific BDSM activities.

This contract and its collection of rules is based on the Dominant being male and the submissive/slave being female.

The term "*slave*" in this book is used interchangeably with the terms "*sub*" and "*submissive*".

The term "*Dominant*" is used interchangeably with "*Master*".

Dominants may wish to test their submissive\slave on how well she remembers the rules.

For FemDomme and female slave relationship, perhaps you'd prefer the contract and book: *"Mistress/slave Contract Incorporating The Ultimate Collection of S&M and BDSM Rules For Female Submissives and Slaves"*.

Please note, these rules are not presented in order of their importance.

Trust, care, mutual consent, safe sex practices, and general safety are absolute priorities. No matter what it's suggested that you incorporate at least the following into your playtime and lifestyle:

- Don't tie things around someone's neck, and no breath play, period!
- Create a "Safe word" for the submissive to say when (or if) things get too scary.
- Always be careful and take necessary safety precautions when engaging in BDSM activity. Keep proper medical facilities handy.
- Always insure that a bound person has adequate circulation. If the person tied up has to go to the bathroom or has physical problems, that person must be immediately released from bondage.
- Ask about medical issues before playing and adjust your playing activities according to any medical issues.
- Never leave anyone bound and alone.
- Understand what a gagged person sounds like in sexual ecstasy versus in pain.
- Do not play while under the influence of drugs or alcohol.
- Always check that your handcuffs and/or lock keys work before playing. If you have to go to the locksmith to get the handcuffs off, it's going to be embarrassing.
- When removing someone from bondage, allow them to move their own limbs.
- If pregnant or ill, check with your doctor before engaging in BDSM related activity.
- Always play within your own skill base and comfort level.

This collection is only a guide. You should add, subtract and adapt rules as desired. There is ample room for that. If you live with others, such as children, it's likely many rules will at least need to be adapted.

Master/slave BDSM Contract

(Feel free to change and adapt those areas of the contract as you see fit.)

I, ____ (slave),
(Print your name)

hereinafter referred to as "**girl**", agree to submit to:

____ (Master),
(Print your name)

hereinafter referred to as "**Master**".

The girl understands that her submission is voluntary and includes sexual submission, BDSM play including bondage and discipline subject to the terms and conditions set forth in this contract.

The girl and her Master agree to the terms as stated in this contract.

Having read and understood this contract, the Master and slave sign this contract freely and without reservation.

The term (length) of this contract is for ____________________ days from the date of signing.

____

MASTER DATE

____

SLAVE DATE

____

Witness (optional) DATE

____

Witness (optional) DATE

A. Rules Governing *Time In* and *Time Out of this Contract*

Definition of Time In: "Time In" refers to the period of time the girl is subject to terms and conditions of this contract. *Time In* is to be considered in effect at all times when the girl is in the Master's presence or communicating with him in any way.

Definition of Time Out: "Time Out" refers to specific periods of time when the girl is **not** subject to the terms and conditions of this contract. The following rules apply to this "*Time Out*" period:

1. Master may call a "Time Out" any time he wishes.

2. (This "time out" can be for a specific period of time or an open-ended period of time.)

3. The girl may request a "Time Out" for a specific period of time only. The girl must state her reasons and the time period for the request and await her Master's permission for the Time Out. Should her Master not grant the Time Out, her only option is to end her relationship with her Master.

B. Master/slave Dynamics *(Written from the perspective of the slave) (Make changes by (1) crossing out the rule and writing into the contract its substitute in the blank space at the end of this section or (2) just crossing out the wording and writing in the new word or words above or below it. (Using white-out and writing over the white-out is an alternative also.)*

1. When Master speaks in person or online in chat, I will stop talking or typing immediately.

2. When in private, I will **always** call Him "Master" or "Sir".

3. Unless not allowed to by my Master, in public I will put my hand around his arm to show we are a couple. Master may instead want us to hold hands.

4. I may not leave a conversation on the Internet or on the phone between myself and my Master without explaining what I need to do first and getting permission from my Master to leave. This is not the case if I'm cut off by the phone or Internet connection.

5. I, the slave will write down and keep on file any new rules Master adds to this list.

6. I will always answer immediately and sincerely every question that Master asks me.

7. I will always show my respect for my Master when in public. I want others to see how important my Master is to me.

When around vanilla strangers that I'll never see again it's ok to call Him (my Master) "Sir", but around family or regular vanilla friends, I call Him by his name. (In summary, I will address Master by his name if I absolutely need to use a name; it's preferable that I use no name to address Master and only call him "Sir" or "Master" but using his name is okay if necessary.)

In the vanilla world, Master cannot require me to call him or someone else in public by a title or name that would humiliate me. (I am the judge of what would humiliate me.) That can include calling Him "Master" in public.

8. Master's slave may not lie about her Master to others and vice versa.

9. I (the slave) am not allowed to lie *to* my Master or be dishonest with him, ever. If master asks me a question I will answer with complete honesty even though I think it could get me punished.

10. While with Master I will make a concerted effort to always look sexy for, and to act seductive with, my Master. My body after all is there for his pleasure.

11. I will try to avoid looking at my Master's eyes straight on.

12. Sitting at the same level as my Master is to be avoided if possible. However in public this is difficult to.

13. Whenever I'm to be played with or otherwise taken, I will immediately take the position my Master orders me to be in.

14. It is my responsibility to clean off all sex toys with rubbing alcohol, soap and water after we use them.

15. I am never allowed to get out of any of my binds without permission when I'm being (or have been) tied up. The obvious exception is if there is an emergency, I am in undue pain and/or I am in some way in danger and/or in a position that puts me in danger.

16. Whenever I'm to be played with or otherwise taken, I will immediately take the position my Master orders me to be in.

17. If I wish to say something to my Master that could be controversial or seem too forward, I will first ask for "*permission to speak freely*".

C. *What I (the slave, i.e. the girl) Will Wear* *(Written from the perspective of the slave) (Make changes by (1) crossing out the rule and writing into the contract its substitute in the blank space at the end of this section or (2) just crossing out the wording and writing in the new word or words above or below it. (Using white-out and writing over the white-out is an alternative also.)*

1. Master has the final say on what I wear when I am with him and that includes when we are in public and in private. In private with my Master I should feel uncomfortable when fully clothed. I am in essence hiding myself from him. The exceptions to this would be if we're expecting company and/or if it's cold.

2. Master can decide what I'm going to wear even though we're not going to be together at that time period. What I wear however must not humiliate me or be a danger to me.

3. I am required to dress feminine at all times unless ordered not to. The exception would be if I need to dress differently for work or another public/vanilla activity of some sort.

4. Nothing loose! I will look sexy at all times. I will wear make-up. I know how important giving pleasure to my Master is and looking sexy gives Master pleasure.

5. I may *never* wear panties while in Master's dwelling (or our mutual home), except to take them off when entering, and in preparation to go out. Of course the exception is when I'm given permission to.

6. I wear dresses or skirts only unless granted permission otherwise. My schoolgirl outfit and other types of BDSM role play outfits should always be ready to wear.

7. When in private, (alone with Master,) if I want to put any clothing on, even a bra or panties, I will ask permission from my Master first.

D. *Rights of the girl (the slave).* *(Make changes by (1) crossing out the rule and writing into the contract its substitute in the blank space at the end of this section or (2) just crossing out the wording and writing in the new word or words above or below it. (Using white-out and writing over the white-out is an alternative also.)*

1. The girl has the right to expect her Master to love, cherish and safeguard her well-being during the period of this contract.

2. The girl has the right to *privacy*. She will not be required to exhibit or provide her submissiveness and/or naked body to others unless she has given full and knowledgeable consent to her Master.

3. Only those who she chooses to be made aware of this contract and/or any of its contents, will be made aware of it. This includes family, friends, business associates and neighbors.

4. The girl reserves the right to decide who may or may not be made aware of this contract, her interest in BDSM and her submission to her Master.

5. The girl has the right to expect her Master to be knowledgeable in the Dominant/submissive lifestyle and to ensure her safety and well-being while participating in any physical activity.

6. *The girl has the right to refuse to participate in any activity, at anytime, which she feels will cause her harm, jeopardize her safety or cause her emotional stress.*

7. The girl has the right to expect that the requirements of her Master will take into consideration her lifestyle and her business situation and adjust to them accordingly.

8. The girl has the right to ask for an adjustment or modification to the terms of this contract at any time. These adjustment(s) must be mutually agreed upon with her Master or the girl's only recourse is to agree to not require said adjustment(s) or modification(s) or instead to terminate the relationship with her Master.

9. The girl and Master have the right to cancel this contract at any time with a simple notification to the other.

10. The girl has to right to expect her Master to both know her, who she is and has always been, and to respect these facets of her personality and not to require her to do or become anything which would make her uncomfortable or in any way interfere with those facets of her personality.

11. When around vanilla strangers that the girl never see again it's ok to call Him (my Master) "Sir", but around family or regular vanilla friends, the girl calls Him by his name. (In summary, the girl will address Master by his name if she absolutely needs to use a name; it's preferable that she will use no name to address Master and only call him "Sir" or "Master" but using his name is okay if necessary.)

In the vanilla world, Master cannot require the girl to call him or someone else in public by a title or name that would humiliate the girl. (The girl is the judge of what would humiliate her.) That can include calling Him "Master" in public.

12. The girl's Master may not steal from her and/or force her to commit an unlawful act.

13. Master may not steal from the girl and/or force the girl to commit an unlawful act.

14. Master's slave may not steal from him and/or force him to commit an unlawful act.

15. Master may not legally and/or illegally take advantage of his slave financially.

16. Master's slave may not legally or illegally take advantage of her Master financially.

17. Financial slavery is never allowed on any occasion.

E. How I (the Slave, i.e. the girl) Will Treat My Body *(Make changes by (1) crossing out the rule and writing into the contract its substitute in the blank space at the end of this section or (2) just crossing out the wording and writing in the new word or words above or below it. (Using white-out and writing over the white-out is an alternative also.)*

1. I (the slave) will always treat my body well and protect it as it exists for my Master's pleasure and to harm it is not only bad for me but disrespectful of my Master. I will need permission from my Master to smoke cigarettes, do drugs, eat poorly, get too little sleep and/or other dangerous activities. For Instance, if I am cooking, I am required to wear an apron to protect my body, even if Master is not allowing me to wear clothing at that time. (*Any Master that does not want his slave to protect her naked body around hot food is likely a bad Master and likely not a good Master to belong to!*)

2. At anytime if Master feels I am no longer the most desirable weight, he can order me to actively lose weight. I will have to go on a diet and/or workout. He can be the taskmaster concerning this and punish me if I am not trying to lose weight. Exceptions will be if I am pregnant or overweight due to a medical condition.

F. Kissing *(Make changes by (1) crossing out the rule and writing into the contract its substitute in the blank space at the end of this section or (2) just crossing out the wording and writing in the new word or words above or below it. (Using white-out and writing over the white-out is an alternative also.)*

1. Master may kiss me on any part of my body anytime he wishes *other than when it could embarrass or humiliate me.* If I don't want Master to kiss me in front of my family, co-workers or boss, etc. then Master is not allowed to. In private Master may kiss any part of my body that He wishes and at anytime and as often as He wishes.

G. Rules Affecting Me Sexually As a Slave *(Make changes by (1) crossing out the rule and writing into the contract its substitute in the blank space at the end of this section or (2) just crossing out the wording and writing in the new word or words above or below it. (Using white-out and writing over the white-out is an alternative also.)*

1. In private, Master may remove (or have me remove) any or all of my clothing at anytime. As a slave, when in private with your Master, you should feel at least somewhat uncomfortable clothed as you are hiding yourself from your Master.

2. My pussy should *always* be kept clean and fresh when with my Master. After all Master may wish to use it for his pleasure at anytime. If Master checks and my pussy is not smelling and/or tasting fresh and clean then I can expect to be punished.

3. I will exercise my pussy to keep it tight for Master's pleasure. I can be punished if my pussy is not tight enough.

While Master is taking me, he may order me to "tighten my pussy" for a short time as he takes me. Master should feel at least some difference in pussy tightness as he is taking me.

My pussy being tighter than most will be a source of pride for me and Master will reward me for having and keeping a tight pussy!

4. When I'm being played with and at the same time Master orders me to cum, I will do so. I will cum longer or harder at Master's discretion. This called "Orgasm-on-demand" and may require some training. When I orgasm, I orgasm for my Master. By orgasming I show Him that I respect Him and that I know I must obey Him. As His slave, when I'm being played with, I have no choice but to orgasm often and as hard as my Master orders.

5. I may not touch my Master's cock and/or balls *ever* without his permission.

6. When kneeling in front of Master, my eyes will be on His cock, my legs at least somewhat spread and hands on His thighs, rubbing His thighs sensually and with great anticipation.

7. When I am in bed with my Master, and if he is awake, I will need permission from my Master to leave the bed.

8. When I and my Master are laying down for rest or sleep, I must lay in a way to always hold and caress His testicles unless Master orders me differently.

9. Unless told otherwise, while Master is sexually playing with me, *I must always ask my Master for permission to cum* unless I have already been given permission to start my orgasm.

Also, unless told otherwise, while Master is sexually playing with me, *I must always ask my Master for permission to **STOP** cumming* unless I have already been given permission to stop my orgasm.

10. While Master is taking me, I will orgasm especially hard when Master is orgasming.

11. When sucking on Master's cock and drinking down my Master's ejaculate as He cums, I will continue sucking on his cock until there is **no** more cum coming out....That will likely be several minutes after he has finished his main orgasm. **I may not touch the tip of Master's cock with my mouth or tongue as he orgasms and after he orgasms for a number of minutes, as it gets very sensitive.** *Should I fail to swallow any of my Master's cum, I will be punished.*

12. My body exists to please my Master - I must always be anxious to cum for my Master.

13. When alone with Master, unless he has told me to do otherwise, I am to ask to suck down his cock's ooze every 30 minutes or so if we're playing, every 60 minutes or so if we're not. Master may want me to continue sucking longer on his cock at that time. If Master is taking me, this rule does not apply.

14. It is always Master who determines how long and how often I suck on his cock, not me. The exception is if I am physically injured in a way that affects the fellatio (such as my mouth is cramping up.)

15. NO teeth to ever be felt on Master's cock EVER or I'll receive dozens of very hard spanks on my very deserving bottom, then I will resume sucking on my Master's cock. This can be repeated an unlimited number of times.

16. If Master says "**head up**" while I am sucking on his cock, I will stop sucking on his cock and pull my mouth off of his cock and wait for his next command.

17. When told to keep my eyes down, I will look only at His cock, whether He is clothed or not, until told otherwise. Master will say "released" or something like it, then I may raise my eyes and go about my business.

18. When I am sucking my Master's cock I may never stop without permission. When just cleaning my master's cock of any ooze, I will suck it dry for a minimum of around 2 minutes. *I don't need permission to stop cleaning my master's cock of ooze if that is all I'm doing.*

19. When I've been ordered to cum, I don't need to ask permission to cum when I'm ready to start my orgasm.

20. When spending the night, or more than a couple of hours in bed with my Master, I may not leave the bed before asking to suck on my Master's cock first (unless Master gives me permission to otherwise leave the bed.)

21. I'm not required to do this regularly but should my Master order me to, I will thank Him for allowing me to cum after I have orgasmed.

22. When my Master's hand moves toward my pussy I will always instinctively spread my legs.

23. When my Master's hand moves toward my breasts I will instinctively move my arms and stick out my chest to make my breasts as available as possible, as they belong to my Master and are there for His pleasure.

24. When in private, if Master wants any of his friends to spank me, while clothed or in my panties, I will comply and not resist during the spanking. I have the final say if this friend will spank me on my bare bottom. If the spanking is too hard and/or that person is disrespectful, I have the right to end this experience at anytime.

25. Master may on occasion, order me to give a friend a hand job and I will comply. The man may only play with my naked breasts during that time (unless I wish otherwise). I do not need to kiss him if I don't wish it.

H. Cunningilus of the slave *(Make changes by (1) crossing out the rule and writing into the contract its substitute in the blank space at the end of this section or (2) just crossing out the wording and writing in the new word or words above or below it. (Using white-out and writing over the white-out is an alternative also.)*

1. *Option 1*: Master will not eat my pussy as part of sex. Master would only eats my pussy as a reward, or as a special occasion such as a celebration. Having my pussy eaten is something I earn. When Master eats my pussy I will orgasm especially hard from it.

2. *Option 2*: Master likes my pussy juice and his slave will be required to provide Him with as much pussy juice as He demands. When in private, at anytime, Master may say "pussy juice" or something like "I want pussy juice" and his slave will quickly remove her cloths from at least her waist down and take a position where it is easiest for her Master to lap down her pussy juice.

As long as they're in private, *when* a slave's pussy will be played with, including eaten, is the Master's decision not the slave's. Her job is to keep her pussy clean and fresh and available.

If the slave is so rude as to not provide her Master with an adequate amount of pussy juice, (and it is her Master not her that will determine if it's an adequate amount), then she will have earned herself punishment. The slave's body exists to give her Master pleasure so refusing to do such a thing is not allowed.

I. *Fellatio & Cock Worship* *(Make changes by (1) crossing out the rule and writing into the contract its substitute in the blank space at the end of this section or (2) just crossing out the wording and writing in the new word or words above or below it. (Using white-out and writing over the white-out is an alternative also.)*

1. If we are in private and I am healthy, I will always obey my Master's order to suck on his cock.

2. The length of time I suck on his cock is up to Him. Literally how I suck on his cock is also up to Him. If any of my body parts is in pain from this activity, I will stop and tell Master about it. He will them allow me to rest. Should Master not allow me to rest, chances are he is a bad Master and I need to find another Master.

3. *Cock Worship* - If I determine I have the free time in life and if Master okays it, I will spend perhaps hours at a time, kissing, sucking, licking, looking at, touching and loving Masters cock and balls. I'm doing this for relaxation so I may think of other things about my life as I do it. Master's pleasure is not a priority during this.

Perhaps this is best considered a form of meditation. Master may be watching television, resting or reading. I will be in my own little world, worshiping Master's cock.

J. The Collar *(Make changes by (1) crossing out the rule and writing into the contract its substitute in the blank space at the end of this section or (2) just crossing out the wording and writing in the new word or words above or below it. (Using white-out and writing over the white-out is an alternative also.)*

1. There is the private collar and the public collar. No one needs to know that the public collar is anything more than a necklace. My public collar could be a vanilla looking necklace but the private collar would clearly be a BDSM collar meant to aid in our playtime.

2. I will wear my public collar at all times other than perhaps when showering or when I need to temporarily wear something else for a special occasion.

3. When in private, Master decides when I should wear my private collar versus my public collar. If Master has not said anything regarding this, or has not previously made a rule about it, I will continue to wear my public collar in private.

K. Spankings *(Make changes by (1) crossing out the rule and writing into the contract its substitute in the blank space at the end of this section or (2) just crossing out the wording and writing in the new word or words above or below it. (Using white-out and writing over the white-out is an alternative also.)*

A normal, good quality spanking will leave a slave's bottom a nice shade of red. This is what a slave should expect, if not hope for. If necessary however, such a spanking should be worked up to.

1. Being spanked is a very important part of my relationship with Master, as well as therapeutic for me as a slave. I will beg Master to spank me often. I will have favorite implements to be spanked by so if Master allows me to pick an implement to be spanked by, I will be ready to bring it to him. When ordered to I will beg to be spanked and afterwards thank Master for taking the trouble of spanking me.

2. I will without hesitation take any position my Master orders me to should He wish to take me, spank me or otherwise play with me or punish me. I am never allowed to block my Master's spanks or try to get away from a position my Master has ordered me to be in unless there is an emergency or I am in harm's way. Should Master ever spank my hand because it was blocking a blow, I will be spanked much harder and longer and perhaps have my hands bound in front of me, if they are not already. I will also have the humiliation of knowing I was so disrespectful.

3. Whenever I and/or Master and I come back from being in the public, I am to ask for a "returning from the public spanking."

4. My pussy must be wet within 60 seconds into any spanking. No spanking will ever end until my pussy is wet.

5. If Master wishes he will train me to orgasm from being spanked. Most slaves can be trained to orgasm from being spanked and as a respectful slave I will learn to orgasm for my Master while being spanked. Within 120 seconds of being spanked, I will naturally start to orgasm (asking Master for permission to cum first of course). Also Master can instead *order me* to start my orgasm during the spanking at anytime 120 seconds or longer into the spanking. As always I will need permission to stop my orgasm assuming I am still being spanked.

For training me to cum from being spanked, Master will likely start by using a vibrator on me during the spanking and ordering me to start orgasming just as he starts the vibrator that's on my clitoris.

Master acknowledges that I may need up to 10 training sessions with a vibrator in this manner. After then, should I disrespect my Master by not cumming while being spanked, (assuming I was given permission to cum,) then I will be punished.

6. During a spanking I may never try to block the blows or try to leave the position He has put me in. When I'm being bound I will not resist, however when I am being bound I may always tell my Master that it hurts (if it hurts) so he can make any necessary changes.

7. Whenever I am to leave the house (apartment or where ever) for more than just quickly going to the car, or something quick of that nature, whether I'm also leaving with Master or not, I will ask my Master for a "going out in the public spanking." This is over and above any other spankings I may have recently received.

8. When alone with Master, unless he has told me to do otherwise, I am to ask every hour, at the beginning of the hour, to be spanked for "my hourly spanking," no matter whether I've been spanked recently or not. Master may not want to spank me but I'm required to ask roughly on the start of each hour anyway.

9. Any crying I do while being spanked (if I need to cry at all) will simply be a turn on for my Master and will not affect the length or to an extent, intensity of my punishment. If I cry while being punished it likely means I'm learning my lesson. The exception is when I'm experiencing physical pain from other correctable sources. For instances if my hands are tied and my shoulder is in a painful position, I should always feel free to tell Master about that and Master is obligated to immediately take me out of the situation that caused me that pain. Reasonable pain from being spanked however is not something that can be negotiated (assuming this point has been agreed upon by both parties.) If I do not like the kind of pain my Master ever gives me directly from being spanked, I need to find another Master or leave the BDSM lifestyle. My Master however should rarely be putting me in that position.

10. The duration and intensity of a spanking and what my Master uses on my bottom is always the choice of my Master. I may however discuss something that concerns me at anytime regarding this.

11. When Master and I are together, if I feel that I am getting into a bad mood, I'm to immediately ask for a "mood correction spanking" from my Master. This rule is repeated every five minutes until the mood changes. Should Master think I need yet another mood correction spanking and I fail to ask for another spanking within 5 minutes, I will receive a caning instead.

12. No blood or blisters from being spanked or otherwise beaten. If something of that nature occurs by accident it can be forgiven by the slave if she wishes. It also depends on how fragile the slave's body is.

13. I must give my okay for Master to spank me anywhere other than my buttocks. (See separate rules concerning flogging my breasts.) I acknowledge that sometimes my upper legs will get spanked as well as my buttocks and I give my okay to that.

L. Foreplay *(Make changes by (1) crossing out the rule and writing into the contract its substitute in the blank space at the end of this section or (2) just crossing out the wording and writing in the new word or words above or below it. (Using white-out and writing over the white-out is an alternative also.)*

1. As He prepares to take me or otherwise have me for his pleasure, Master determines what our foreplay will be. I am allowed to make suggestions as to what to include in foreplay and always allowed to tell Master if something makes me uncomfortable or hurts.

Master might like me to kneel naked on the floor by the bed in preparation for me to taken. I'll remove his clothing when ordered to, climb on the bed and give Master a massage, including a butt massage. Again Master determines how long I massage any part of Him.

Master may then turn over and I will turn my attention to Master's penis when ordered to.

M. Miscellaneous Physical (including sexual) Orders I (the girl, i.e. the slave) Will Obey

(Make changes by (1) crossing out the rule and writing into the contract its substitute in the blank space at the end of this section or (2) just crossing out the wording and writing in the new word or words above or below it. (Using white-out and writing over the white-out is an alternative also.)

1. When I am laying on my stomach for any reason and my Master says "elbows", I am to raise my upper body up on my elbows so my breasts are readily available to my Master to reach under my torso and play with. My elbows must not block access to my breasts. My breasts after all are my Master's property.

2. While with Master, if my Master ever says "kneel in front of the bed", unless he points out a particular spot to kneel at, I am to automatically assume I am to immediately go to the pad on the floor next to the bed and kneel on it waiting for his further instructions. My eyes are to be looking down on the bed and staying that way until Master releases me.

If Master just says "kneel" I will kneel in front of him wherever he is and wait for his next instructions. My eyes will be on his cock (or his clothed midsection) as I hope to be sucking it soon.

N. Anal Sex *(Make changes by (1) crossing out the rule and writing into the contract its substitute in the blank space at the end of this section or (2) just crossing out the wording and writing in the new word or words above or below it. (Using white-out and writing over the white-out is an alternative also.)*

1. Once I have given my Master permission to take me anally in our relationship, he may take me anally (after I'm lubed up real well) at anytime. I have the right at anytime to require Master to put more lubrication in my anus and/or on his cock if I feel there is not enough lubrication. Master may never re-enter my pussy after entering my anus prior to being cleaned very well, as infections can occur that way. The rule is that once Master enters my anus with his cock, his cock may not re-enter my vagina and mouth unless I have thoroughly cleaned his pubic area to my full satisfaction.

2. Master may insert toys into my anus as he plays with me but no toy touching my anus may be used for any other purpose until I have cleaned it thoroughly with rubbing alcohol, soap and water.

3. Master may inset a (finger for finger-fucking) into my anus if his finger nail is well manicured and clipped and it will not harm my anus.

O. Pussy unshaved, unshaven and if unshaved, it's appearance *(Make changes by (1) crossing out the rule and writing into the contract its substitute in the blank space at the end of this section or (2) just crossing out the wording and writing in the new word or words above or below it. (Using white-out and writing over the white-out is an alternative also.)*

1. It is Master's decision on whether his slave's pussy is shaved or unshaved, trimmed or untrimmed and if trimmed to what extent and what the design is. The slave has final say in regard to any waxing.

P. Play Rape *(Make changes by (1) crossing out the rule and writing into the contract its substitute in the blank space at the end of this section or (2) just crossing out the wording and writing in the new word or words above or below it. (Using white-out and writing over the white-out is an alternative also.)*

1. I hereby give Master permission to include *Play Rape* at any point during our playtimes. I will not resist unless ordered to as that could give Master the wrong impression as to if I'm enjoying it or not it. Master likely will require me to resist only from the waist up as he is holding me down taking me. I likely will also be bound as he takes me.

Q. Breast Bondage & Related *(Make changes by (1) crossing out the rule and writing into the contract its substitute in the blank space at the end of this section or (2) just crossing out the wording and writing in the new word or words above or below it. (Using white-out and writing over the white-out is an alternative also.)*

1. In private Master has access to my breasts at anytime. I will take whatever position Master orders me to so as to make my breasts more easily and readily accessible to Him.

2. When Master flogs my breasts I expect my nipples to become erect, my breasts to perhaps become some shade of red and tender if flogged for a lengthy period. I understand that flogging my breasts may become an integral part of our playtime. *I have the final say as to what Master can spank my breasts with and how long my breasts are spanked.*

No blood or blisters. Unless I bruise easily (which often also means the bruises go away quickly also,) bruising is to be avoided with any playtime activity.

3. Master may use my breasts for breast bondage but Master must release my breasts from bondage completely at anytime that I wish.

4. If I allow it, Master may drip melted wax on my naked breasts as I am tied down (or in any position that he wants.)

R. Punishments *(Make changes by (1) crossing out the rule and writing into the contract its substitute in the blank space at the end of this section or (2) just crossing out the wording and writing in the new word or words above or below it. (Using white-out and writing over the white-out is an alternative also.)*

A list can be added here.

S. *Medical Play* *(Make changes by (1) crossing out the rule and writing into the contract its substitute in the blank space at the end of this section or (2) just crossing out the wording and writing in the new word or words above or below it. (Using white-out and writing over the white-out is an alternative also.)*

Safe medical scenes/gyno play utilizing the slave as the patient is allowed whenever the Master wants it but the slave has the final say on what can be done to her.

T. Showering and Bathing *(Make changes by (1) crossing out the rule and writing into the contract its substitute in the blank space at the end of this section or (2) just crossing out the wording and writing in the new word or words above or below it. (Using white-out and writing over the white-out is an alternative also.)*

1. Master may order me to shower or take a bath *at anytime* that he wishes.

2. Master may order me to shower or bath *with him* at anytime that he wishes.

3. I cannot be ordered by Master to bath with another person if I don't want to.

4. If I am bathing or showering with Master, he has the right to require me to scrub him or otherwise bath him or play with him as to his specifications. Master may bath me as he wishes, assuming it does not put me in danger.

U. Massaging Master *(Make changes by (1) crossing out the rule and writing into the contract its substitute in the blank space at the end of this section or (2) just crossing out the wording and writing in the new word or words above or below it. (Using white-out and writing over the white-out is an alternative also.)*

1. If in private, at anytime, Master can order me to massage him in wherever way he wishes. Master determines the length of the massage, its intensity, what body part I massage and what I'll be wearing (or not wearing) while massaging. I will get used to giving Master likes long butt massages!

V. Corner Time *(Make changes by (1) crossing out the rule and writing into the contract its substitute in the blank space at the end of this section or (2) just crossing out the wording and writing in the new word or words above or below it. (Using white-out and writing over the white-out is an alternative also.)*

1. When my Master requires me to do corner time, I will be positioned in the corner, naked unless otherwise decided by my Master. I will go there without resisting.

If possible my hands may be tied together to a hook on the ceiling above my head, and my legs tied to a leg spreader bar. I may or may not be spanked during corner time and I may or may not be required to cum for my Master during corner time. My Master will determine how long my corner time is and how often I am to be spanked while there and how often I will be required to cum, if at all.

If I have to go to the bathroom or have physical problems, Master is required to release me from bondage.

W. Pulling Out Individual Pubic Hairs as Punishment *(Make changes by (1) crossing out the rule and writing into the contract its substitute in the blank space at the end of this section or (2) just crossing out the wording and writing in the new word or words above or below it. (Using white-out and writing over the white-out is an alternative also.)*

1. As punishment, if I allow it, Master, using a tweezers and magnifying glass, can pull out individual pubic hairs. I may or may not be tied down in place.

X. Unacceptable Behavior of the slave which includes Jealousy, Pouting, Being Bitchy, Slovenly and Lazy *(Make changes by (1) crossing out the rule and writing into the contract its substitute in the blank space at the end of this section or (2) just crossing out the wording and writing in the new word or words above or below it. (Using white-out and writing over the white-out is an alternative also.)*

1. Master always has the right to punish me if He thinks I deserve it. Acting in the above manner will be a recipe for punishment.

Y. Master Having Multiple Slaves *(Make changes by (1) crossing out the rule and writing into the contract its substitute in the blank space at the end of this section or (2) just crossing out the wording and writing in the new word or words above or below it. (Using white-out and writing over the white-out is an alternative also.)*

1. If I agree to it, Master may have multiple female slaves, of which I am one.

2. Once I agree to it, when in private, Master can order me to play with his other slave(s) in the manner that he wishes. Master can also have play/have sex with us all at the same time (and separately) if the proper sanitation and contraceptive precautions are being adhered to.

3. I will not be jealous of the attention the other slave(s) gets which includes Master's sexual favors. I will expect to be punished if I get jealous of Master giving my sister slave(s) attention.

---

4. If I am playing with the other slave I will take her pleasure and needs very seriously, as she is also required to do with me.

5. All Master's slaves may need permission to play with each other. Sometimes I will be the dominant person when playing with the other slave and vice versa.

6. I will care about my sister slave(s) as well as my Master.

Z. Having Sex and playing with Others Besides Master

If I allow it, others at my Master's discretion may kiss me, touch and/or otherwise play with my sexual private parts as my Master sees fit. If I allow it, Master *may* order me to suck on somebody's cock, eat their pussy, have intercourse with them, make out with them, kiss them or bath them.

If I allow it, others at my Master's discretion may use me for purposes of BDSM play.

AA. Objectification (Objectification is requiring the slave to act like an object, such as a footstool.) *(Make changes by (1) crossing out the rule and writing into the contract its substitute in the blank space at the end of this section or (2) just crossing out the wording and writing in the new word or words above or below it. (Using white-out and writing over the white-out is an alternative also.)*

If allowed, provide more specifics here:

BB. *Mummification* (full plastic wrap) (This is the wrapping of the slave's body in plastic film [Saran Wrap type] from below the neck down to as far as the toes.) *(Make changes by (1) crossing out the rule and writing into the contract its substitute in the blank space at the end of this section or (2) just crossing out the wording and writing in the new word or words above or below it. (Using white-out and writing over the white-out is an alternative also.)*

Mummification of the slave is allows at her Master's discretion.

CC. *Blind Folds* *(Make changes by (1) crossing out the rule and writing into the contract its substitute in the blank space at the end of this section or (2) just crossing out the wording and writing in the new word or words above or below it. (Using white-out and writing over the white-out is an alternative also.)*

The use of a blindfold on the slave by her Master can be done on each occasion only when the slave allows it.

DD. *Pin Wheel Use* *(Make changes by (1) crossing out the rule and writing into the contract its substitute in the blank space at the end of this section or (2) just crossing out the wording and writing in the new word or words above or below it. (Using white-out and writing over the white-out is an alternative also.)*

Judicial use of the Wattenberg wheel (Pin Wheel) use on the slave's is allowed except for the following areas of her body:

a) anywhere in her pussy,
b) anyway from the neck up,
c) her knees

d)

e)

EE. *Crossplaying* (Crossplaying is where the slave is bound naked or otherwise to a large wooden cross and the Master does with her as he wishes.) *(Make changes by (1) crossing out the rule and writing into the contract its substitute in the blank space at the end of this section or (2) just crossing out the wording and writing in the new word or words above or below it. (Using white-out and writing over the white-out is an alternative also.)*

Safe crossplaying is allowed as Master desires it.

FF. *Orgasm Denial* *(Make changes by (1) crossing out the rule and writing into the contract its substitute in the blank space at the end of this section or (2) just crossing out the wording and writing in the new word or words above or below it. (Using white-out and writing over the white-out is an alternative also.)*

Orgasm Denial of His slave is allowed to be done periodically by her Master.

GG. *Cock worship* and ***Butt worship*** *(Make changes by (1) crossing out the rule and writing into the contract its substitute in the blank space at the end of this section or (2) just crossing out the wording and writing in the new word or words above or below it. (Using white-out and writing over the white-out is an alternative also.)*

The slave will perform this on her Master whenever he wishes.

HH. *Maid Service* *(Make changes by (1) crossing out the rule and writing into the contract its substitute in the blank space at the end of this section or (2) just crossing out the wording and writing in the new word or words above or below it. (Using white-out and writing over the white-out is an alternative also.)*

Maid service will be provided at least semi-regularly by the slave if her Master wants it.

II. ***Gags*** *(Make changes by (1) crossing out the rule and writing into the contract its substitute in the blank space at the end of this section or (2) just crossing out the wording and writing in the new word or words above or below it. (Using white-out and writing over the white-out is an alternative also.)*

Master may only use a gag on his slave when his slave allowed it. His slave must okay each instance of it.

JJ. *Strap-on Dildos & Vibrators* *(Make changes by (1) crossing out the rule and writing into the contract its substitute in the blank space at the end of this section or (2) just crossing out the wording and writing in the new word or words above or below it. (Using white-out and writing over the white-out is an alternative also.)*

Judicial use of strap-on dildos and vibrators **are allowed** on the slave as well as when taking the slave in her pussy and ass. If the strap-on touches or enters her anus, it may not be used on her in any way until it is thoroughly cleaned off as it is no sanitary anymore.

KK. *Master Being Taken with a Dildo/vibrator* *(Make changes by (1) crossing out the rule and writing into the contract its substitute in the blank space at the end of this section or (2) just crossing out the wording and writing in the new word or words above or below it. (Using white-out and writing over the white-out is an alternative also.)*

If master wishes it, his slave **will** use a strap-on to take him in his anus while she jerks him off and/or performs fellatio on him.

LL. *Handcuffs, Chains and Shackles* *(Make changes by (1) crossing out the rule and writing into the contract its substitute in the blank space at the end of this section or (2) just crossing out the wording and writing in the new word or words above or below it. (Using white-out and writing over the white-out is an alternative also.)*

Handcuffing, chaining and shackling of the slave for purposes of bondage **is** allowed if done safely and in private. If not in private, the slave must okay it on each occurrence.

MM. *Deepthroating* *(Make changes by (1) crossing out the rule and writing into the contract its substitute in the blank space at the end of this section or (2) just crossing out the wording and writing in the new word or words above or below it. (Using white-out and writing over the white-out is an alternative also.)*

The slave **will** learn to and perform deepthroating of Master's cock. The slave will deep throat Master's cock when he wishes.

NN. *Leather, Rubber or Latex Clothing* *(Make changes by (1) crossing out the rule and writing into the contract its substitute in the blank space at the end of this section or (2) just crossing out the wording and writing in the new word or words above or below it. (Using white-out and writing over the white-out is an alternative also.)*

1. Master may require his slave to wear leather, rubber or latex clothing.

OO. *Role Playing* *(Make changes by (1) crossing out the rule and writing into the contract its substitute in the blank space at the end of this section or (2) just crossing out the wording and writing in the new word or words above or below it. (Using white-out and writing over the white-out is an alternative also.)*

Role playing (RP) is allowed. Allowable role playing scenarios are to be written in below. When the role playing will begin is always at the Master's discretion. (*Any additional RP scenarios can be added at later times with both parties signing and dating the additions.*)

1. When in private with her Master, and in a safe and private environment, and at her Master's discretion, the slave is required to wear any role play outfit Master wants her to and is available to them. This includes school girl outfits, nursing uniform, etc.

2. Master will always have the final word as to how the role play outfit is worn.

Role Play Scenarios

A)

B)

C)

D)

E)

PP. Cumming From Performing Fellatio on Master's Cock *(Make changes by (1) crossing out the rule and writing into the contract its substitute in the blank space at the end of this section or (2) just crossing out the wording and writing in the new word or words above or below it. (Using white-out and writing over the white-out is an alternative also.)*

1. If Master requires it, his slave will train herself to orgasm from just performing fellatio on her Master's cock. Master must give her an adequate training period, including using a vibrator on her while she is performing fellatio but at some point if the slave is not cumming from fellatio alone, she should expect to be punished.

QQ. Birth Control *(Make changes by (1) crossing out the rule and writing into the contract its substitute in the blank space at the end of this section or (2) just crossing out the wording and writing in the new word or words above or below it. (Using white-out and writing over the white-out is an alternative also.)*

1. The slave promises to actively and aggressively guard her body from unwanted pregnancy.

RR. Tattoos, Branding, Piercing *(Make changes by (1) crossing out the rule and writing into the contract its substitute in the blank space at the end of this section or (2) just crossing out the wording and writing in the new word or words above or below it. (Using white-out and writing over the white-out is an alternative also.)*

1. I as the slave will always have the final decision on whether I am going to have on my body any tattoos, branding, piercing or any other type of semi-permanent or permanent physical alterations. However, if I want to do any of the previously mentioned, *but* my Master doesn't want me to do it, then I am not allowed to do it. Thus if I want to have a piercing but my Master won't allow it, I will not be able to get that piercing.

SS. *None of the below activities are allowed without the consent (on each occasion) of both parties:*

Erotic Dance
Defilement,
Seeing a Partner Dirty or Wet
Exhibitionism/Sex in Public
Furry
Hair Pulling
High Heels
Hunt-and-Capture
Lace/Lingerie
Leather
Making Home
Masks
Podophilia (Foot Fetish)
Sissification
Urolagnia (Water Sports/Urine)
Voyeurism
Tickling
Blood play
Knife play
Breath control (breathplay, asphyxiation)
Scat play
Urine play
Collar and Lead/Leash
Hypnosis of the submissive
Forced cross-dressing
Forced homosexuality or bi-sexuality of the submissive
Nipple torture
Spitting on the submissive
Toilet play
Diaper play (Master's submissive may not be required to wear a diaper.)
Needle play
Electric Play (*Tens, Violet Wand and Shock devices*)
CBT (cock and ball torture)
Boot worship by the submissive of her Master's boots
Kissing of clean boots/shoes of others
Verbal abuse
Ashtray play (When the submissive makes herself like a table so her Master can put an ashtray on her back.)
Forced chastity
Sensory deprivation
Suspension/suspension play
Humiliation
Daddy/daughter
Forced 24/7 servitude of the submissive.
Public exhibition of a submissive
Pain enhancement of the submissive
Ponygirl play (where the submissives pretends to be a pony, is dressed up as such and ridden.)
Duct tape use on the submissive
Purposely stretching of any part of the submissive's body
Forced confinement of the submissive
Total Power Exchange (TPE) - (TPE is loosely defined as one person [the Master] completely, utterly and totally making the decisions for himself and his submissive.)
Unusual mind control games

Rimming (licking, eating, and/or otherwise using the mouth/tongue on/in her Master's anus).
Fisting of the submissive's pussy
Fisting of the submissive's anus
Pantyhose/Stockings
Participating in Erotic Photography
Pinching
Pussy-Whipping
Tit-shocking
Bestiality (This is illegal. Don't do it.)

ADDITIONAL RULES

Great BDSM Suggested Playtime Scenario

The following could be a typical playtime scenario for you young lady and your Master.

1. When you enter my (our) place, you will take off your shoes and go kneel on the thick padding next to my bed (or other agreed upon spot like a chair or couch). Unless told otherwise, your eyes will be looking at where my midsection would be when I sit down in front of you. You will wait for me there (unless of course I'm already there.)

2. I will come over and sit in front of you (assuming I'm not already there.) I may or may not have clothes on. You'll then put your hands on my upper legs, massaging my legs with anticipation. Keep your hands high up on my legs, massaging my legs but you may not touch my penis until allowed to.

3. I will kiss you, touch you, play with you, talk to you and undress you as you kneel submissively in front of me. At some point you may be ordered to stand up and take the rest of your clothes off. Unless you're told differently, in private, as a slave you should feel uncomfortable with clothes hiding your private parts from your Master. They exist for his pleasure afterall!

4. You will partially or fully undress me when I order you to. When you pull my pants and underwear down, you know what will pop out!

5. I will then let you suck on my penis. You will first likely have to beg for it though. Also, remember to always play with Master's testicles while you suck…always!

   Rule: Never let any of Master's penis' ooze go to waste. You know good it tastes! Beg Master to let you check for ooze often! Keep sucking Master's ooze down until he allows you to stop.

6. Soon I will reach down and play with your exposed, vulnerable breasts as you suck on my penis.

7. At some point I may order you to stop sucking my penis. If so I will tie your hands securely together.

8. I may order you to suck on my penis again or we will go straight to the following:

   I will sit further back on the bed (or couch/chair) and you will lay stomach down across my lap. I will give you a nice sensual spanking, playing with your body as I do.

   I will then tell you to get up and we will go to the bed (if we're not already there.) I will set the bed up so I am sitting with my back against the headboard of the bed and you are laying in front of me face-down on cushions with your head positioned so you can easily suck on my penis and play with my scrotum using your tied-together hands. If I do that though I will make sure there is enough slack in the rope for your hands to still move freely around my penis and scrotum while you suck. If your hands are tied to the middle of the headboard in this manner, I will be sitting on the rope as my butt will be in-between your bound hands and the headboard which your hands are tied to.

9. I'll also put a roughly 4' x 3' (though it can be larger) sheet of plastic under your upper body to keep the massage lotion or oil from going on the bed covers. (More on this massage very soon!)

   Your breasts will now be positioned, thanks to cushions, so the bottom tips (which will likely be the nipples) of the breasts are just above the bed. As you are lying down and sucking on my penis, I will **generously** lubricate (and keep lubricated,) your breasts with some brand of preferably non-desensitizing lotion or massage oil. (I prefer lotion. Baby lotions at dollar stores often are good ones to try but lotions can vary by brand.) The longer the lotion can stay viscous, the better. If warming is necessary (which it most likely will be,) I will warm the lotion/oil up ahead of time or rub it in my hands to warm it up. I will then massage your breasts as you suck on my penis and play with my testicles.

I will continue for a long time to massage your lubricated breasts as you suck on my penis. (This is known as "*Extreme Pleasure Breast Massage*".) **Remember massagers, always keep you're your hands well lubricated!**

Massager and massagee will quickly notice that the nipples respond with the most pleasure from this type of massage. The Dom will find that massaging his slave's breast's large fleshy area first for a while will be quite pleasurable to his slave but it is still not near as pleasurable as briskly massaging her nipples with a circular twisting motion that lets the fingers slide firmly over the nipple, not actually twisting it.

I will first make my slave beg to have her nipples massaged using this *Extreme Pleasure Breast Massage* technique. My slave has no more than 30 seconds to start her orgasm when I first start giving her *Extreme Pleasure Breast Massage.* Once I start massaging her nipples, she will have to orgasm a lot harder or risk being punished.

Using a yardstick type implement, I can also reach across your back and spank your bottom as you suck. Obviously one should make sure the woman can handle being spanked while sucking. Most can depending on the intensity of the spanking and how hard she's already orgasming.

Optional: After doing this for some time, you may wish for the lovely lady to be turned over on her back, her hands still tied to the bed. The man can then eat her. The lady should plan on providing her Master or Mistress a lot of pussy juice. Should she not provide you with enough pussy juice, feel free to turn her over so her bottom is facing up, and give her a good spanking. Then try eating her again. (Before playing it is important that the lady keep her pussy clean and fresh.) After you've had your fill of her pussy juice, both of you can go back to the original position mentioned in this section or move on to #10.

10. At some point, I may also tie each foot to its corresponding corner of the bed. Instead I may tie your feet securely together and then tie them to the middle of the bed frame at the foot of the bed. Don't worry guys, the placement of a woman's vagina on her body while she's laying on her stomach is such that you still most likely will have easy access even with her legs closed. (This could be a problem depending on how overweight she and/or he is.)

11. At some point I will order you to stop sucking by saying "head up". I will then get up and give you another spanking as you lay tied down, just for good measure. If you've been a good girl and are getting a lot of pleasure from all this, *and if you beg for it*, I will put a special vibrator (or two) inside and/or on you and set it up so it stays in place. (Tight underwear and white first aid fabric tape often works best where there are pubic hairs in the area.) I will then return to my original position on the bed and you will continue sucking me and I will also continue giving you *Extreme Pleasure Breast Massage* (which I promise you'll enjoy immensely!) I will continue to periodically spank you with a yardstick type implement as described earlier.

12. After a while, I will order you to stop sucking. I'll then clean the lotion off your breasts with a small towel(s) and remove the small plastic sheet that caught lotion that came off your breasts and my hands. I'll also remove the cushions from under you that kept your breasts just above the bed. You are now comfortably laying face down on the bed but now without the cushions and plastic under you. You still however are tied down to the bed as you lie on your stomach. (You may wish to put a clean towel under her breasts if they are still a bit oily from the massage.) I will remove any vibrators on and/or in you, as well as whatever was holding them in place. You will be completely naked, tied down, helpless and ready to be taken.

13. I will come back in front of you and order you to suck on my penis again. After it is hard, I will dry it off and put a condom on it. I will then lay on top of you, stomach down, and enter you with my thick penis.

14. As I take you, you will orgasm for as long as I order you to and orgasm as hard as I order you to. You are required, as part of the orgasm on demand training, to start orgasming within 5 seconds of me entering you. Believe me it is much easier than it may sound. You will need to ask for permission to start orgasming though! As long as you start asking for permission within 5 seconds of me entering you, you are doing fine. Of course you will need permission to stop your orgasm also! There is the possibility that at some point I will order you to

stop your orgasm during our lengthy playtime (or obviously you may have to do that due to unexpected events like the kids coming home early.) If you can however, you are welcome to keep orgasming even though direct sexual stimulation has temporarily stopped; (for instances after I have stopped taking you.) Once direct sexual stimulation of your breasts and your vagina restarts, you'll of course have to re-start your orgasm once again (assuming it had stopped,) and within 5 seconds as always. (Many of the ladies I have trained will continue orgasming for many minutes after physical sexual stimulation has stopped.)

15. As I take you, you will orgasm for as long as I order you to and orgasm as hard as I order you to. Believe me young lady, I require long, hard orgasms from you.

16. As you know I am taking you while both of us are on our stomachs. My stomach of course is on your back. This is far and away the main position I will take you in for the entire time I take you. I may also take you doggie style depending on how overweight the slave is. There will however not be an emphasis on multiple sex positions during our playtime.

    RULE: while I'm playing with you, if you are lying on your stomach and if I ever say "elbows" you are to raise your chest enough so that the tips of your lovely breasts are just above the bed, thus making it easier for me to play with your breasts by sliding one or more of my hands under your chest as I am taking you.

    (I think you'll find that *my stomach on your back position* to be a very good one. Depending on how heavy and/or tall the guy is, you won't have any trouble breathing as my weight is well distributed over your bone-protected pelvis. You won't have to deal with my breathing on your face or you being pounded against the headboard like in the missionary position. Also I can hold you tightly as I take you and easily talk to you as my mouth can be right by your ear.

17. At some point I will slide one or both of my arms under your underarm(s) and put my hands on or around your hands. I am now securely holding you down with my hands. You can now reach my hands (as they are on your wrist, forearms or hands) and kiss them should that be our desire.

    RULE: while we are playing you will only address me as "Sir" or "Master".

18. Sometimes while I am taking you like this, I will spank you. This is accomplished best by me holding myself up with one hand/arm while I am in you and then spanking you with a paddle or the like with the other hand.

19. Often I will hold you down while I take you. I will order you to struggle *FROM THE WAIST UP* to get free as I am holding you down and taking you at the same time. We will do this one or more times during our long playtime.

20. Sometimes I will take you faster than other times. You will get even more pleasure from this as most any woman would.

21. Sometimes I will thrust into you as deep and hard as I can. You will get even more pleasure from this as most any woman would.

22. This is an excellent sex position for a lady to be taken anally. Perhaps she should have her anus lubed in the beginning when she is originally laid in place incase her Master/Mistress decides to take her anally.

    RULE: *Remember, the man must always wear a condom when taking her anally and he* ***can not*** *re-enter her vagina unless his pubic area has been thoroughly cleaned. A bladder infection is just one of the problems she can have if one doesn't abide by this essential safety tip.*

Remember, if something is hurting young lady, you need to tell your Master immediately so he can stop.

END

47138716R00024

Made in the USA
Middletown, DE
17 August 2017